8/01

Trees

Ernestine Giesecke

Heinemann Library
Des Plaines, Illinois

Designed by Lindaanne Donohoe
Printed in Hong Kong

03 02 01 00 99
10 9 8 7 6 5 4 3 2 1

Library of Congress Cataloging-in-Publication Data

Giesecke, Ernestine, 1945–
Trees/Ernestine Giesecke.
    p.   cm. — (Outside my window)
    Includes bibliographical references and index.
    Summary: Introduces and explains the characteristics of trees and shows how to find
and identify a variety of North American trees.
    ISBN 1-57572-684-X (lib. bdg.)
    1. Trees—Juvenile literature. [1. Trees.] I. Title. II.
Series: Giesecke, Ernestine, 1945– Outside my window.
QK475.8.G54 1998
582.16—dc21

98-6362
CIP
AC

Acknowledgments

The publisher would like to thank the following for permission to reproduce copyright photographs:

Cover: Tony Stone Images, Inc./Rich Iwasaki

Phil Martin, pp. 4, 8, 16, 17, 22, back cover; Tony Stone Images, Inc./Willard Clay, p. 5; Earth
Scenes/Richard Shiell, pp. 6, 14, 19; Earth Scenes/Ted Levin, p. 7; Tony Stone Images, Inc./Ernnest
Braun, p. 9 top; Tristan Boyer, pp. 9 bottom, 11 bottom; Tony Stone Images, Inc./Rich Iwasaki, p. 10;
Tony Stone Images, Inc./Stuart Westmorland, p.11 top; Earth Scenes/Leonard Lee Rue III, p.12;
Earth Scenes/Donald Specker, p.13; Oxford Scientific Films/David Wrigglesworth, p. 15; First Image
West, Inc./Bernadette Heath, p.18 top; Grant Heilman, p.18 bottom; Earth Scenes/Patti Murray,
p. 19 insert; First Image West, Inc./Steve Bruno, p. 20; Earth Scenes/C.C. Lockwood, p. 21.

Every effort has been made to contact copyright holders of any material reproduced in this book.
Any omissions will be rectified in subsequent printings if notice is given to the publisher.

Some words are shown in bold, **like this.** You can find out what they mean by looking in the glossary.
The glossary word **Circumference** is in every "More About. . ." box, but is shown in bold only in the first box.

Contents

13.95

Outside Your Window

You can learn about nature by looking out your window. Look for something old and wild.

Then find something that makes shade and grows taller every year.

Look closely at trees. They are part of nature.
Notice that some trees are different from
others. This book will help you learn about
the trees you may see outside your window.

What is a Tree?

A tree is a large woody plant. Trees use sunlight, water, and soil to grow big and strong.

flower

leaves

branch

trunk

You can tell one kind of tree from another by comparing the parts of the trees.

The roots of a tree bring water and food from the soil. The bark acts like skin. It protects the inside of the tree. Leaves use sunlight to make the food that a tree needs to grow.

Oak

An oak tree has many, many leaves in summer. Each leaf has a wavy edge. In fall, the leaves fall from the tree. During winter, this kind of oak tree has no leaves.

If you look on the ground under an oak tree, you will find **acorns.** Inside an acorn is the seed of an oak tree. After many years of water, sun, and soil, the **seedling** will grow to be a tall, strong tree.

MORE ABOUT OAKS

- Height: 80 to 100 feet (24 to 30 m)
- **Circumference:** 6 feet (2 m)
- Acorns are food for birds and mammals.

Maple

This is a maple tree. Each maple leaf is wide and shaped like a hand. Maple leaves are green in spring and summer. In fall, maple leaves turn red, yellow, and gold.

You will find maple seeds in **pairs.** They look like wings. They are carried away from the tree by the wind. Some of the seeds will fall where they can grow.

MORE ABOUT MAPLES

- Height: 75 to 100 feet (23 to 30 m)
- Circumference: 2 to 4 feet (1 to 1 1/2 m)
- Maple syrup is made from the sap of maple trees.

Sumac

Sumac trees are short and have fuzzy branches. Look for old and young sumac trees near one another. Roots of an old tree spread away from the tree. These roots can become **sprouts.** Soon a young tree grows and makes its own roots.

The leaf of a sumac tree is made of many small parts. Each part is called a *leaflet*. All the leaflets look alike. Birds and some small animals eat the bright fruits of the sumac tree.

MORE
ABOUT
SUMAC

- Height:
  20 feet (6 m)

- Circumference:
  4 inches
  (10 cm)

- Berries are
  food for birds
  and mammals

13

Crab Apple

Crab apple trees have flowers that grow into fruit. In spring, crab apple trees are covered with white or pink flowers. The flowers have a sweet smell. They last about two weeks before falling off.

In late summer and early fall, the fruit is ready to be picked. Inside the crab apple fruit are the seeds of new trees. These small crab apples are in the same family as the apples you eat.

MORE ABOUT CRAB APPLES

- Height: 15 to 30 feet (5 to 9 m)
- Circumference: 2 to 4 feet (1 to 1 1/2 m)
- Crab apples are used to make jams and jellies.

Pine

Pine trees have very thin, narrow leaves called needles. A pine tree, like other evergreens, does not lose its needles in fall. A needle may stay on the tree for three or four years.

Look for **cones** on pine trees. The seeds for new pine trees are inside closed cones. The cones open in warm weather and the wind carries the seeds away. Some seeds reach places that are just right for growing new pine trees.

MORE ABOUT PINES

- Height: 80 to 110 feet (24 to 34 m)

- Circumference: 2 to 4 feet (1 to 1 1/2 m)

- Wood is used to build houses and furniture.

Poplar

These are the leaves and seeds of one kind of poplar tree. There are tiny hairs around the seed. The wind will carry the seeds away from the tree. This tree is called a *cottonwood* tree because its seeds look like the seeds of cotton plants.

The bark of this poplar tree is different from the bark of other trees. It is gray. It has ridges like tiny mountains. Poplar trees grow very fast. Some can grow five feet in one year.

MORE ABOUT POPLARS

- Height: 75 to 100 feet (23 to 30 m)

- Circumference: 3 to 6 feet (1 to 2 m)

- Wood is used to make boxes, matches, and paper.

Joshua Tree

MORE ABOUT JOSHUA TREES

- Height: 15 to 30 feet (5 to 9 m)

- Circumference: 1 to 3 feet (30 cm to 1 m)

- One of the only trees to grow in deserts.

You will find the Joshua tree where it is nearly always hot and dry. The leaves of the tree are stiff and full of water. They have a special shape. Any water they catch runs back to the trunk of the tree.

Bald Cypress

This tree grows in **swamps** and **marshy** places. The tree looks like it has spikes. These spikes are roots that grow above the wet ground and water so they can breathe.

MORE ABOUT BALD CYPRESSES

- Height: 80 to 120 feet (24 to 37 m)
- Circumference: 3 to 4 feet (1 to 1 1/2 m)
- Wood is used for railroad ties, posts, and roofs.

Tree Scrapbook

1. Make a rubbing of tree bark and collect some of the leaves. Do this for different trees.

2. Paste the rubbing and leaves into your scrapbook.

3. Write the name of the tree in your scrapbook.

Glossary

acorns   nuts that are the seeds of an oak tree

circumference   distance around a tree trunk

cones   protective cases for pine tree seeds

marshy   wet, soft land

pairs   in twos, like twins

seedling   beginnings of a new plant

sprouts   young plant

swamps   wet, spongy lands sometimes covered with water

More Books to Read

Burns, Diane. *Trees, Leaves and Bark*. Milwaukee: Gareth Stevens, 1998.

Feltwell, John. *Trees*. New York: DK Publishing, 1997.

Lyon, George. *A B Cedar: An Alphabet of Trees*. New York: Orchard Books, 1996.

Trees in This Book

Index